Assize Sermon on National Apostasy

National Apostasy

considered in a Sermon preached
in St. Mary's Church, Oxford
before His Majesty's Judges of Assize
on Sunday July 14th 1833 by

The Rev. John Keble M.A.

with an introduction by
The Rev. Dr. Alan Stephenson

THE ROCKET PRESS

Privately printed and published for July 1983 by
The Rocket Press at The Vicarage, Steventon,
Abingdon, Oxfordshire - in association with the
1983 Oxford Movement Celebrations Committee.

Introduction © Alan M. G. Stephenson 1983
Illustrations © John R. Smith 1983

ISBN 0 946676 00 3

John Keble 1792 - 1866

1815 Deacon   1816 Priest
1817 Tutor at Oriel College, Oxford
1827 *The Christian Year* published
1831 Professor of Poetry at Oxford
1833 *National Apostasy* first published
1836 Vicar of Hursley in Hampshire
1866 Died at Bournemouth, March 29th
1870 Keble College founded in Oxford

Introduction

John Keble's sermon delivered on the appointment of the Vice-Chancellor of Oxford, in St. Mary's Church, before the Judges of the Assize is famous not because it was a brilliant piece of eloquence which set people talking, but because it was regarded by John Henry Newman as the start of the Oxford or Tractarian Movement. In his *Apologia Pro Vita Sua* Newman wrote, 'I have ever considered and kept the day as the start of the religious movement of 1833.' Earlier he had written, 'The true and primary author of it, however, as is usual with great motive-powers, was out of sight. Having carried off as a mere boy the highest honours of the university, he had turned from the admiration which haunted his steps, and sought for a better and holier satisfaction in pastoral work in the country. Need I say that I am speaking of John Keble?'

The occasion of the sermon was the threat (soon a fact) by the British Parliament to curtail by ten the number of Anglican bishoprics in Ireland, where the number of members of the United Church of England and Ireland was decidedly limited. We today see this government action as a sensible and necessary piece of ecclesiastical reform, but Keble saw it as gross erastianism; and his message is one of 'Let the State get its hands off the Church.'

The sermon is hardly scintillating, but Keble's sermons never were; he believed that brilliant sermons attracted attention away from the Christian message to the preacher. Consequently he was often dull, and made no apology for that.

The sermon caused no great stir at the time and there do not appear to be any vivid reminiscences of it. *Jackson's Oxford Journal* reported a large congregation but no national newspaper lauded it as obviously heralding a new movement at Oxford or in the church. It was little noticed.

9

But Keble published it under the title *National Apostasy* and sent copies of it to his friends. One of the two judges who heard it is said to have remarked that 'it was an appropriate discourse.' Some barristers of the Tory party thought it too strong, especially as one of the judges, Sir John Gurney, was (or had been) a Dissenter. J. B. Mozley in the Preface to his *Essays Historical and Theological* remarked, 'I cannot help thinking it a kind of exordium of a great revolution – shall I call it? – coming on, whether rapidly or slowly we cannot tell, but at any rate most surely.' What did Pusey have to say about the sermon? 'It is possible,' wrote Liddon, 'that Pusey heard the sermon; but no record of his sense of the importance of the manifesto survives. The copy of the published sermon which was sent him "from the author" remains uncut.'

The essential message of the sermon is that the Church of England represents here the Universal Catholic Church, with its episcopal ministry going back to the Apostles. Its founder was Christ, not Parliament. This message was put more brilliantly and more flamboyantly in Newman's Tract 1, which came out later in the same year.

ALAN M.G. STEPHENSON

Preface to the First Edition

Since the following pages were prepared for the press, the calamity, in anticipation of which they were written, has actually overtaken this portion of the Church of God. The Legislature of England and Ireland, (*the members of which are not even bound to profess belief in the Atonement,*) this body has virtually usurped the commission of those whom our Saviour entrusted with *at least one voice* in making ecclesiastical laws, on matters wholly or partly spiritual.[1] The same Legislature has also ratified, to its full extent, this principle; – that the Apostolical Church in this realm is henceforth only to stand, in the eye of the State, as *one sect among many*, depending, for any pre-eminence she may still appear to retain, merely upon the accident of her having a strong party in the country.

It is a moment, surely, full of deep solicitude to all those members of the Church who still believe her authority divine, and the oaths and obligations, by which they are bound to her, undissolved and indissoluble by calculations of human expediency. Their anxiety turns not so much on the consequences, to the State, of what has been done, (*they* are but too evident,) as on the line of conduct which they are bound themselves to pursue. How may they continue their communion with the Church *established*, (hitherto the pride and comfort of their lives,) without any taint of those Erastian Principles on which she is now avowedly to be governed? What answer can we make henceforth to the partisans of the Bishop of Rome, when they taunt us with being a mere Parliamentarian Church? And how, consistently with our present relations to the State, can even the doctrinal purity and integrity of the MOST SACRED ORDER be preserved?

The attention of all who love the Church is most earnestly solicited to these questions. They are such, it will be observed, as cannot be answered by appealing to precedents in English History, because, at most, such could only shew, that the difficulty might have been raised before. It is believed, that there are hundreds, nay thousands, of Christians, and that soon there will be tens of thousands, unaffectedly anxious to be rightly guided with regard to these and similar points. And they are mooted thus publicly, for the chance of eliciting, from competent judges, a correct and early opinion.

If, under such trying and delicate circumstances, one could venture to be positive about any thing, it would seem safe to say, that in such measure as it may be thought incumbent on the Church, or on Churchmen, to submit to any profane intrusion, it must at least be their sacred duty, to declare, promulgate, and record, their full conviction, that it *is* intrusion; that they yield to it as they might to any other tyranny, but do from their hearts deprecate and abjure it. This seems the least that can be done: unless we would have our children's children say, 'There was once here a glorious Church, but it was betrayed into the hands of Libertines for the real or affected love of a little temporary peace and good order.'

JOHN KEBLE July 22nd 1833

National Apostasy

As for me, God forbid that I should sin against the Lord
in ceasing to pray for you: but I will teach you the good
and the right way. 1 SAMUEL 12: 23

On public occasions, such as the present, the minds of
Christians naturally revert to that portion of Holy Scripture,
which exhibits to us the will of the Sovereign of the world
in more immediate relation to the civil and national conduct of mankind. We naturally turn to the Old Testament,
when public duties, public errors, and public dangers, are
in question. And what in such cases is natural and obvious,
is sure to be more or less right and reasonable. Unquestion-
ably it is a mistaken theology, which would debar Christian
nations and statesmen from the instruction afforded by the
Jewish Scriptures, under a notion, that the circumstances
of that people were altogether peculiar and unique, and
therefore irrelevent to every other case. True, there is hazard
of misapplication, as there is whenever men teach by example. There is peculiar hazard, from the sacredness and
delicacy of the subject; since dealing with things supernatural and miraculous as if they were ordinary human
precedents, would be not only unwise, but profane. But
these hazards are more than counterbalanced by the absolute
certainty, peculiar to this history, that what is there com-
mended was right, and what is there blamed, wrong. And
they would be effectually obviated, if men would be careful
to keep in view this caution: – suggested every where, if I
mistake not, by the manner in which the Old Testament
is quoted in the New: – that, as regards reward and punishment, God dealt formerly with the Jewish people in a manner analogous to that in which He deals now, not so much
with Christian nations, as with the souls of individual
Christians.

Let us only make due allowances for this cardinal point of difference, and we need not surely hesitate to avail ourselves, as the time may require, of those national warnings, which fill the records of the elder Church: the less so, as the discrepancy lies rather in what is revealed of God's providence, than in what is required in the way of human duty. Rewards and punishments may be dispensed, visibly at least, with a less even hand; but what tempers, and what conduct, God will ultimately reward and punish, – this is a point which cannot be changed: for it depends not on our circumstances, but on His essential, unvarying Attributes.

I have ventured on these few general observations, because the impatience with which the world endures any remonstrance on religious grounds, is apt to shew itself most daringly, when the Law and the Prophets are appealed to. Without any scruple or ceremony, men give us to understand that they regard the whole as obsolete: thus taking the very opposite ground to that which was preferred by the same class of persons two hundred years ago; but, it may be feared, with much the same purpose and result. Then, the Old Testament was quoted at random for every excess of fanatical pride and cruelty: now, its authority goes for nothing, however clear and striking the analogies may be, which appear to warrant us in referring to it. The two extremes, as usual, meet; and in this very remarkable point: that they both avail themselves of the supernatural parts of the Jewish revelation to turn away attention from that, which they, of course, most dread and dislike in it: its authoritative confirmation of the plain dictates of conscience in matters of civil wisdom and duty.

That portion, in particular, of the history of the chosen people, which drew from Samuel, the truest of patriots, the wise and noble sentiment in the text, must ever be an unpleasing and perplexing page of Scripture, to those, who would fain persuade themselves, that a nation, even a Christian nation, may do well enough, as such, without

God, and without His Church. For what if the Jews were bound to the Almighty by ties common to no other people? What if He had condescended to know them in a way in which He was as yet unrevealed to all families of the earth besides? What if, as their relation to Him was nearer, and their ingratitude more surpassing, so they might expect more exemplary punishment? Still, after all has been said, to exaggerate their guilt, in degree, beyond what is supposed possible in any nation whatever now, what can it come to, in kind and in substance, but only this; – that they rejected God? that they wished themselves rid of the moral restraint implied in His peculiar presence and covenant? They said, what the prophet Ezekiel, long after, represents their worthy posterity as saying, 'We will be as the heathen, the families of the countries.'[2] Once for all, we will get rid of these disagreeable, unfashionable scruples, which throw us behind, as we think, in the race of worldly honour and profit.' Is this indeed a tone of thought, which Christian nations cannot fall into? Or, if they should, has it ceased to be displeasing to God? In other words, has He forgotten to be angry with impiety and practical atheism? Either this must be affirmed, or men must own, (what is clear at once to plain unsophisticated readers,) that this first overt act, which began the downfall of the Jewish nation, stands on record, with its fatal consequences, for a perpetual warning to all nations, as well as to all individual Christians, who, having accepted God for their King, allow themselves to be weary of subjection to Him, and think they should be happier if they were freer, and more like the rest of the world.

I do not enter into the question, whether visible temporal judgments are to be looked for by Christian nations, transgressing as those Jews did. Surely common sense and piety unite, in representing this inquiry as, practically, one of no great importance. When it is once known for certain that such and such conduct is displeasing to the King of kings, surely common sense and piety concur in setting their mark of reprobation on such conduct, whether the punishment, sure to overtake it, come to-morrow, or a year hence, or wait till we are in another world.

Waving this question, therefore, I proceed to others, which appear to me, I own, at the present moment especially, of the very gravest practical import.

What are the symptoms, by which one may judge most fairly, whether or no a nation, as such, is becoming alienated from God and Christ?

And what are the particular duties of sincere Christians, whose lot is cast by Divine Providence in a time of such dire calamity?

The conduct of the Jews, in asking for a king, may furnish an ample illustration of the first point: the behaviour of Samuel, then and afterwards, supplies as perfect a pattern of the second, as can well be expected from human nature.

(1) The case is at least possible, of a nation, having for centuries acknowledged, as an essential part of its theory of government, that, as a Christian nation, she is also a part of Christ's Church, and bound, in all her legislation and policy, by the fundamental rules of that Church – the case is, I say, conceivable, of a government and people, so constituted, deliberately throwing off the restraint, which in many respects such a principle would impose on them, nay, disavowing the principle itself; and that, on the plea, that other states, as flourishing or more so in regard of wealth and dominion, do well enough without it. Is not this desiring, like the Jews, to have an earthly king over them, when the Lord their God is their King? Is it not saying in other words, 'We will be as the heathen, the families of the countries,' the aliens to the Church of our Redeemer?

To such a change, whenever it takes place, the immediate impulse will probably be given by some pretence of danger from without, – such as, at the time now spoken of, was furnished to the Israelites by an incursion of the children of Ammon; or by some wrong or grievance in the executive government, such as the malversation of Samuel's sons, to whom he had deputed his judicial functions. Pretences will never be hard to find; but, in reality, the movement will always be traceable to the same decay or want of faith, the same deficiency in Christian resignation and thankfulness, which leads so many, as individuals, to disdain and forfeit the blessings of the Gospel. Men not impressed with religious principle attribute their ill success in life, – the hard times they have to struggle with, – to any thing rather than their own ill-desert: and the institutions of the country, ecclesiastical and civil, are always at hand to bear the blame of whatever seems to be going amiss. Thus, the discontent in Samuel's time, which led the Israelites to demand a change of constitution, was discerned by the Unerring Eye, though perhaps little suspected by themselves, to be no better than a fresh development of the same restless, godless spirit, which had led them so often into idolatry. 'They have not rejected thee, but they have rejected Me, that I should not reign over them. According to all the works, which they have done since the day that I brought them up out of Egypt even unto this day, wherewith they have forsaken Me, and served other gods, so do they also unto thee.'[3]

The charge might perhaps surprise many of them, just as, in other times and countries, the impatient patrons of innovation are surprised, at finding themselves rebuked on religious grounds. Perhaps the Jews pleaded the express countenance, which the words of their Law, in one place,[4] seemed, by anticipation, to lend to the measure they were urging. And so, in modern times, when liberties are to be taken, and the intrusive passions of men to be indulged, precedent and permission, or what sounds like them, may be easily found and quoted for every thing. But Samuel, in God's name, silenced all this, giving them to understand, that in His sight the whole was a question of motive and purpose, not of ostensible and colourable argument; – in

His sight, I say, to Whom we, as well as they, are nationally responsible for much more than the soundness of our deductions as matter of disputation, or of law; we are responsible for the meaning and temper in which we deal with His Holy Church, established among us for the salvation of our souls.

These, which have been hitherto mentioned as omens and tokens of an Apostate Mind in a nation, have been suggested by the portion itself of sacred history, to which I have ventured to direct your attention. There are one or two more, which the nature of the subject, and the palpable tendency of things around us, will not allow to be passed over.

One of the most alarming, as a symptom, is the growing indifference, in which men indulge themselves, to other men's religious sentiments. Under the guise of charity and toleration we are come almost to this pass; that no difference, in matters of faith, is to disqualify for our approbation and confidence, whether in public or domestic life. Can we conceal it from ourselves, that every year the practice is becoming more common, of trusting men unreservedly in the most delicate and important matters, without one serious inquiry, whether they do not hold principles which make it impossible for them to be loyal to their Creator, Redeemer, and Sanctifier? Are not offices conferred, partnerships formed, intimacies courted, – nay, (what is almost too painful to think of,) do not parents commit their children to be educated, do they not encourage them to intermarry, in houses, on which Apostolical Authority would rather teach them to set a mark, as unfit to be entered by a faithful servant of Christ?

I do not now speak of public measures only or chiefly; many things of that kind may be thought, whether wisely or no, to become from time to time necessary, which are in reality as little desired by those who lend them a seeming concurrence, as they are, in themselves, undesirable. But

I speak of the spirit which leads men to exult in every step of that kind; to congratulate one another on the supposed decay of what they call an exclusive system.

Very different are the feelings with which it seems natural for a true Churchman to regard such a state of things, from those which would arise in his mind on witnessing the mere triumph of any given set of adverse opinions, exaggerated or even heretical as he might deem them. He might feel as melancholy, – he could hardly feel so indignant.

But this is not a becoming place, nor are these safe topics, for the indulgence of mere feeling. The point really to be considered is, whether, according to the coolest estimate, the fashionable liberality of this generation be not ascribable, in a great measure, to the same temper which led the Jews voluntarily to set about degrading themselves to a level with the idolatrous Gentiles? And, if it be true any where, that such enactments are forced on the Legislature by public opinion, is APOSTASY too hard a word to describe the temper of that nation?

The same tendency is still more apparent, because the fair gloss of candour and forbearance is wanting, in the surly or scornful impatience often exhibited, by persons who would regret passing for unbelievers, when Christian motives are suggested, and checks from Christian principles attempted to be enforced on their public conduct. I say, 'their public conduct,' more especially; because in that, I know not how, persons are apt to be more shameless, and readier to avow the irreligion that is in them; – amongst other reasons, probably, from each feeling that he is one of a multitude, and fancying, therefore, that his responsibility is divided.

For example: – whatever be the cause, in this country of late years, (though we are lavish in professions of piety,) there has been observable a growing disinclination, on the part of those bound by VOLUNTARY OATHS, to whatever reminds them of their obligation; a growing disposition to explain it all away. We know what, some years ago, would have been thought of such uneasiness, if betrayed by persons officially sworn, in private, legal, or commercial life. If there be any subjects or occasions, now, on which men are inclined to judge of it more lightly, it concerns them deeply to be quite sure, that they are not indulging or encouraging a profane dislike of God's awful Presence; a general tendency, as a people, to leave Him out of all their thoughts.

They will have the more reason to suspect themselves, in proportion as they see and feel more of that impatience under pastoral authority, which our Saviour Himself has taught us to consider as a never-failing symptom of an unchristian temper. 'He that heareth you, heareth Me; and he that despiseth you, despiseth Me.'[5] Those words of divine truth put beyond all sophistical exception, what common sense would lead us to infer, and what daily experience teaches; – that disrespect to the Successors of the Apostles, as such, is an unquestionable symptom of enmity to Him, Who gave them their commission at first, and has pledged Himself to be with them for ever. Suppose such disrespect general and national, suppose it also avowedly grounded not on any fancied tenet of religion, but on mere human reasons of popularity and expediency, either there is no meaning at all in these emphatic declarations of our Lord, or that nation, how highly soever she may think of her own religion and morality, stands convicted in His sight of a direct disavowal of His Sovereignty.

To this purpose it may be worth noticing, that the ill-fated chief, whom God gave to the Jews, as the prophet tells us, in His anger,[6] and whose disobedience and misery were referred by himself to his 'fearing the people, and obeying their voice,'[7] whose conduct, therefore, may be fairly taken as a sample of what public opinion was at that time supposed to require, – his first step in apostasy was, perhaps, an intrusion on the sacrificial office,[8] certainly an impatient breach of his engagement with Samuel, as the last and greatest of his crimes was persecuting David, whom he well knew to bear God's special commission. God forbid, that any Christian land should ever, by her prevailing temper and policy, revive the memory and likeness of Saul, or incur a sentence of reprobation like his. But if such a thing should be, the crimes of that nation will probably begin in infringement on Apostolical Rights; she will end in persecuting the true Church; and in the several stages of her melancholy career, she will continually be led on from bad to worse by vain endeavours at accommodation and compromise with evil. Sometimes toleration may be the word, as with Saul when he spared the Amalekites; sometimes state security, as when he sought the life of David; sometimes sympathy with popular feeling, as appears to have been the case, when violating solemn treaties, he attempted to exterminate the remnant of the Gibeonites, in his zeal for the children of Israel and Judah.[9] Such are the sad but obvious results of separating religious resignation altogether from men's notions of civil duty.

(2) But here arises the other question, on which it was proposed to say a few words; and with a view to which, indeed, the whole subject must be considered, if it is to lead to any practical improvement. What should be the tenor of their conduct, who find themselves cast on such times of decay and danger? How may a man best reconcile his allegiance to God and his Church with his duty to his country, that country, which now, by the supposition, is fast becoming hostile to the Church, and cannot therefore long be the friend of God?

Now in proportion as any one sees reason to fear that such is, or soon may be, the case in his own land, just so far may he see reason to be thankful, especially if he be called to any national trust, for such a complete pattern of his duty, as he may find in the conduct of Samuel. That combination of sweetness with firmness, of consideration with energy, which constitutes the temper of a perfect public man, was never perhaps so beautifully exemplified. He

21

makes no secret of the bitter grief and dismay, with which the resolution of his countrymen has filled him. He was prepared to resist it at all hazards, had he not received from God Himself directions to give them their own way; protesting, however, in the most distinct and solemn tone, so as to throw the whole blame of what might ensue on their wilfulness. Having so protested, and found them obstinate, he does not therefore at once forsake their service, he continues discharging all the functions they had left him, with a true and loyal, though most heavy, heart. 'God forbid that I should sin against the Lord in ceasing to pray for you: but I will teach you the good and the right way.'

Should it ever happen (which God avert, but we cannot shut our eyes to the danger) that the Apostolical Church should be forsaken, degraded, nay trampled on and despoiled by the State and people of England, I cannot conceive a kinder wish for her, on the part of her most affectionate and dutiful children, than that she may, consistently, act in the spirit of this most noble sentence; nor a course of conduct more likely to be blessed by a restoration to more than her former efficiency. In speaking of the Church, I mean, of course, the laity, as well as the clergy in their three orders, – the whole body of Christians united, according to the will of Jesus Christ, under the Successors of the Apostles. It may, by God's blessing, be of some use, to shew how, in the case supposed, the example of Samuel might guide her collectively, and each of her children individually, down even to minute details of duty.

The Church would, first of all, have to be constant, as before, in INTERCESSION. No despiteful usage, no persecution, could warrant her in ceasing to pray, as did her first fathers and patterns, for the State, and all who are in authority. That duty once well and cordially performed, all other duties, so to speak, are secured. Candour, respectfulness, guarded language, – all that the Apostle meant, in warning men not to 'speak evil of dignities,' may then, and then only, be practised, without compromise of truth and fortitude, when the habit is attained of praying as we ought for the very enemies of our precious and holy cause.

The constant sense of God's presence and consequent certainty of final success, which can be kept up no other way, would also prove an effectual bar against the more silent but hardly less malevolent feeling, of disgust, almost amounting to misanthropy, which is apt to lay hold on sensitive minds, when they see oppression and wrong triumphant on a large scale. The custom of interceding, even for the wicked, will keep the Psalmist's reasoning habitually present to their thoughts: 'Fret not thyself because of the ungodly, neither be thou envious against the evil doers: for they shall soon be cut down like the grass, and be withered even as the green herb... Leave off from wrath, and let go displeasure: fret not thyself, else shalt thou be moved to do evil.'[10]

Thus not only by supernatural aid, which we have warrant of God's word for expecting, but even in the way of natural consequence, the first duty of the Church and of Churchmen, INTERCESSION, sincerely practised, would prepare them for the second; – which, following the words of Samuel as our clue, we may confidently pronounce to be REMONSTRANCE. 'I will teach you the good and the right way.' REMONSTRANCE, calm, distinct, and persevering, in public and in private, direct and indirect, by word, look, and demeanour, is the unequivocal duty of every Christian, according to his opportunities, when the Church landmarks are being broken down.

Among laymen, a deep responsibility would appear to rest on those particularly, whose profession leads them most directly to consider the boundaries of the various rights and duties, which fill the space of civilized Society. The immediate machinery of change must always pass through their hands: and they have also very great power in forming and modifying public opinion. The very solemnity of this day may remind them, even more than others, of the close amity which must ever subsist between equal justice and pure religion; Apostolical religion, more especially, in proportion to her superior truth and exactness. It is an amity, made still more sacred, if possible, in the case of the Church and Law of England, by historical recollections, associations and precedents, of the most engaging and ennobling cast.

But I return to the practical admonition afforded her, in critical periods, by Samuel's example.

After the accomplishment of the change which he deprecated, his whole behaviour, to Saul especially, is a sort of expansion of the sentiment in the text. It is all earnest INTERCESSION with God, grave, respectful, affectionate REMONSTRANCE with the misguided man himself. Saul is boldly rebuked, and that publicly, for his impious liberality in sparing the Amalekites, yet so as not to dishonour him in the presence of the people. Even when it became necessary for God's prophet to shew that he was in earnest, and give the most effectual of warnings, by separating himself from so unworthy a person, – when 'Samuel came no more to see Saul,'[11] – even then, we are told, he still 'mourned for him.'

On the same principle, come what may, we have ill learned the lessons of our Church, if we permit our patriotism to decay, together with the protecting care of the State. 'The powers that be are ordained of God,' whether they foster the true Church or no. Submission and order are still duties. They were so in the days of pagan persecution; and the more of loyal and affectionate feeling we endeavour to mingle with our obedience, the better.

After all, the surest way to uphold or restore our endangered Church will be for each of her anxious children, in his own place and station, to resign himself more thoroughly to his God and Saviour in those duties, public and private, which are not immediately affected by the emergencies of the moment: the daily and hourly duties, I mean, of piety, purity, charity, justice. It will be a consolation understood by every thoughtful Churchman, that let his occupation be, apparently, never so remote from such great interests, it is in his power, by doing all as a Christian, to credit and advance the cause he has most at heart; and what is more, to draw down God's blessing upon it. This ought to be felt, for example, as one motive more to exact punctuality in those duties, personal and official, which the return of an Assize week offers to our practice; one reason more for veracity in witnesses, fairness in pleaders, strict impartiality, self-command, and patience, in those on whom decisions depend; and for an awful sense of God's presence in all. An Apostle once did not disdain to urge good conduct upon his proselytes of lowest condition, upon the ground, that, so doing, they would adorn and recommend the doctrine of God our Saviour.[12] Surely, then, it will be no unworthy principle, if any man be more circumspect in his behaviour, more watchful and fearful of himself, more earnest in his petitions for spiritual aid, from a dread of disparaging the holy name of the English Church, in her hour of peril, by his own personal fault or negligence.

As to those who, either by station or temper, feel themselves most deeply interested, they cannot be too careful in reminding themselves, that one chief danger, in times of change and excitement, arises from their tendency to engross the whole mind. Public concerns, ecclesiastical or civil, will prove indeed ruinous to those, who permit them to occupy all their care and thoughts, neglecting or undervaluing ordinary duties, more especially those of a devotional kind.

These cautions being duly observed, I do not see how any person can devote himself too entirely to the cause of the Apostolical Church in these realms. There may be, as far as he knows, but a very few to sympathise with him. He may have to wait long, and very likely pass out of this world before he see any abatement in the triumph of disorder and irreligion. But, if he be consistent, he possesses, to the utmost, the personal consolations of a good Christian: and as a true Churchman, he has that encouragement, which no other cause in the world can impart in the same degree: – he is calmly, soberly, demonstrably, SURE, that, sooner or later, HIS WILL BE THE WINNING SIDE, and that the victory will be complete, universal, eternal.

He need not fear to look upon the efforts of Antichristian powers, as did the Holy Apostles themselves, who welcomed the first persecution in the words of the Psalmist:

'*Why do the heathen rage, and the people imagine a vain thing?*
The kings of the earth stand up, and the rulers take counsel
together, against the Lord, and against His Anointed.
For of a truth against Thy Holy Child Jesus, Whom Thou
hast anointed, both Herod and Pontius Pilate, with the Gentiles,
and the people of Israel, were gathered together,

FOR TO DO WHATSOEVER THY HAND AND THY COUNSEL DETERMINED BEFORE TO BE DONE.'[13]

References to the text

(1) In the suppression of certain
Irish Sees, *contrary to the suffrage of the Bishops
of England and Ireland.*

(2) Ezekiel 20: 32   (3) 1 Samuel 8: 7,8

(4) Deuteronomy 17: 14 - 20   (5) Luke 10: 16

(6) Hosea 13: 11   (7) 1 Samuel 15: 24

(8) 1 Samuel 13: 8 - 14   (9) 2 Samuel 21: 2

(10) Psalm 37: 1, 2, 8   (11) 1 Samuel 15: 35

(12) Titus 2: 10   (13) Acts 4: 25 - 28

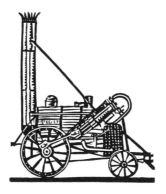

This limited edition of 700 copies has been hand
and machine-set in Baskerville type and printed by
Jonathan Stephenson of The Rocket Press in his
workshop in the former stables at Steventon Vicarage.
The illustration on the cover, of St. Mary's Church
in Oxford, and the frontispiece of John Keble are
both original linocuts by John R. Smith.

THIS IS COPY NUMBER   436